IOO POEMS W

This book was awarded the *International Publishers' Prize* on May 1st 1977 and under the auspices of that body is now being published simultaneously in seven different languages throughout the world. This edition is the first publication in English.

Other books by Erich Fried available in English

On Pain of Seeing (poems)
Last Honours (poems)

100 POEMS WITHOUT A COUNTRY

ERICH FRIED

Translated by Stuart Hood

JOHN CALDER
LONDON

First published in Great Britain in 1978 by
John Calder (Publishers) Ltd
9-15 Neal Street, London WC2H 9TU

Second Impression 1990

British Library Cataloguing in Publication Data is available.
Library of Congress Cataloging in Publication Data is available.

Typeset in Baskerville 11pt by Gloucester Typesetting Co., Gloucester.
Printed in Great Britain by Southampton Book Co, Southampton.

CONTENTS

P²: Poetry about Poetry

Germany—Political

Through the Net

Acknowledgement: The poems asterisked were translated by George
Rapp and first published in the volume, *On Pain of Seeing*.

INTRODUCTION

Exile is hard for anyone to bear. To writers it presents special problems—how to keep in touch with their native language, how to avoid linguistic arrest, how to retain the ability to speak to their fellow-countrymen and women. This collection is called *100 Poems without a Country* because they are the work of a man who was born as a Jew in Vienna, who has lived in London for the last forty years, but who is yet a poet whose work is written for and read by a wide public in the German-speaking lands. This means that, although he moves between two cultural worlds, he has never lost living touch with his native tongue and its literature. This has not always been easy for him. He admits that some of the poetry he wrote during and just after the war showed signs of cultural estrangement from the best and most living traditions in German writing. If today he is known as one of the most important of the engaged poets writing in German it is because he has become, over the years since the war, increasingly involved in the politics of the German Federal Republic. Language is a social artefact. To use it well, to use it so as to be able to speak to others, the writer must be involved in and exposed to the social forces that mould it. That involvement Fried has deliberately sought.

In his case a line can be traced from membership of the post-war literary group—the '47 Group—which disintegrated under the pressure of political developments in western Germany, through active participation in the Extra-Parliamentary Opposition which sprang out of the student movement of the late '60s to his present interventions in the intellectual and political life of a country which is increasingly intolerant of radical thought and expression, increasingly conscious of its role as the dominant capitalist power in Europe. Within Germany Fried's is one of the voices that protest against the policies of the Federal Government—policies which have driven sections of the German intelligentsia into desperate and fatal adventures. It is not that he

ix

is a writer of agit-prop; on the contrary, his work is an example of that 'organic assimilation' of experience which Trotsky maintained distinguished literary activity from political agitation. Fried is a political poet because he thinks and lives politically.

It is inevitable that a poet who aims to make political interventions through his writing should react to events by writing occasional poems aimed at attacking a current idiocy, intended to make a political point or to coin a slogan; of such poems Fried has written a considerable number, which have been extremely effective politically in Germany. They have not been included in this volume because of their ephemeral nature and their local reference. But a taste of what his work in this line is like can be gathered from *Wanted—Animals* which is at once an occasional poem and a telling comment on the dehumanised vocabulary of authority and the alienated attitudes of police officials. His poems on Vietnam or Chile, on the other hand, illustrate the way in which he combines depth of feeling with grasp of political realities. It is precisely the same depth of feeling as informs his personal poems, whether they deal with his fears, his childhood memories, his memories of those of his family who went to the gas-chambers or were shot, or his personal relationships. Fried's poetry is remarkable because it expresses a spectrum of feeling in which there is no dividing-line between the political and the personal. His political attitudes are formed by his attitudes towards his fellow human beings and his reaction to their collective and individual fates. To understand why he is such a remarkable political poet one need only read *What is Life?*—which is a love poem.

I first translated a poem of Erich Fried's in 1944, when I did not know him. Today, after thirty years of friendship, I was able to work on these translations with him. Certain poems we discarded because they are untranslatable. At one time Fried produced a large number of poems—he is very prolific—in which he stretched to the limits the capacity of the German language for word-play. It was a style from which he broke away but he still uses the technique he learned at that time with brilliant but inimitable and untranslatable effect. If those poems which have been chosen succeed at all as translations it is because of the strength of the originals, their essential clarity. They illustrate the work of a poet who is gifted, varied, serious yet capable of wit and humour, a writer with an immense command of language, a Marxist humanist, a very remarkable man.

STUART HOOD
November 1977

FIRST PERSON SINGULAR

Shaving

The sharper the blade
the younger
I look in the mirror

How sharp
must the edge be
that makes me really young?

Fast alles

Ich habe meine Lehrzeit
hinter mir
Ich lernte hören und sehen:
Fast alle Menschen taten
fast allen Menschen
fast alles
       Und fast alle Menschen
       denen fast alles angetan wurde
       sagten dann
       mit fast versagender Stimme:
       'Der Tag wird kommen
Der Tag an dem wir fast allen
fast alles antun werden
was sie uns angetan haben'
Ich hörte sie das selbst sagen
fast wörtlich
       Und solange das
       fast alles ist was sie wollen
       oder fast alles
       was sie wissen von dem was sie wollen
       wird dieser Tag
       von dem sie fast alle fast träumen
       immer wieder nur fast kommen
       nie ganz wirklich
Wirklich
das habe ich gelernt
und möchte fast sagen
so gelernt
daß mir Hören und Sehen verging
Ich habe jetzt meine Lehrzeit
fast hinter mir

Almost Everything

I have my time for learning
behind me
I learned to hear and to see
Almost everybody did
almost everything
to almost everyone
      And almost everyone
      to whom almost everything was done
      said
      with almost failing voice
      'The day will come
the day when we'll do almost everything
that they did to us
to almost everyone'
I heard them say it myself
almost word for word
      And so long as that
      is almost all they want
      and almost all
      they know about what they want
      then that day
      of which they almost all dream
      will always almost come
      never really
Really
that much I have learned
and might almost say
so learned
that my hearing and sight are gone
Now I have my time for learning
almost behind me

Lady World

I came
into the world
and have
at last reached
the point

where I ask
out loud
how I came
to come
into it

She comes
and says softly:
You are not coming
you are already
leaving

Lady World: A reference to the medieval German concept of *Frau Welt*,
who was represented as beautiful from the front but worm-eaten and
ugly when seen from behind.

6

The Flood

I climb the steps to my door
in wet mist
Water rises in the sewers

I climb up
my winding way to school
in the pouring rain
The gutters foam down to the river

I climb up
to the wooded hill north of the town
in the cloudburst
The waves from the plain
tear the grass from the slope

I climb up
into the black beams of the lookout
Irresistibly
the sea falls on me
and overwhelms me

I hold fast
to the boughs of a drifting tree
it rises and falls
with the flood
A weary bird
leaves in its beak
cowers
on a twig

Bird's flesh stills hunger
the bones fall into the sea
Bloody olive-leaves sail
and drift away
feathers drift
and fish fly
I am thirsty

Nostalgie

Kommt zurück ihr Falschspieler!
Ich ziehe den Hut vor euren
verwegenen Schlapphüten
Schirmmützen
struppigen Haaren
Kommt zurück
kommt her
aus euren verregneten oder
versandeten Gräbern
im wilder gewordenen Westen

Kommt zurück ihr Fallensteller der Fallensteller!
Einmal nur kommt noch
Bringt eure gezinkten Karten
das As aus dem Ärmel
die schräggestellte Roulette
eure hohlen Würfel
mit lebendigem Quecksilber drinnen—

Das Spiel geht um nichts
und um nichts hieß
als ich ein Kind war
'um die Ehre'
so wußte ich: 'Ehre ist nichts'

Ihr Falschspieler habt
auf eure Ehre verzichtet
um auf nichts verzichten zu müssen
Da habt ihr richtig gespielt—
bis zum blutigen *happy end* eurer Filme

Einmal noch gönnt mir das alles
ihr Vorläufer!
Wie ich mich sehne
nach der Einfalt eurer Kniffe und kleinen Gewinne
nach der bekämpfbaren Täuschung von Mann zu Mann!

Nostalgia

Come back you card-sharpers
I take my hat off to your
dashing slouched hats
peaked caps
matted hair
Come back
Come here
out of your rain-sodden
or sand-choked graves
in a West grown wilder still

Come back you trappers of trappers
Come just this once
Bring your marked cards
the ace up your sleeves
the tilted roulette wheel
your hollow dice
loaded with lively quicksilver

There are no stakes
and 'no stakes' meant
when I was a child
'for honour'
so I knew: 'Honour is nothing'

You card-sharpers have
sacrificed your honour
so as to sacrifice nothing at all
You picked the right game—
until the bloody happy ending of your films

Once more grant me all this
my forerunners!
How I long
for the simplicity of your ruses and little winnings
for the man-to-man cheating which can be dealt with

Windige Urgroßväter ohne Klimaanlage
ihr würdet staunen an welche Tische gebunden
wir heute zum Falschspiel gezwungen werden
und welche
schwerbewaffneten Spieler gegen uns spielen
nach Regeln die sie ändern
von Karte zu Karte

Und an der Wand steht:
'Nur wer sich wehrt ist ein Mann'
damit sie uns
rechtmäßig abknallen können

Windy forefathers without air-conditioning
you would be amazed how today we are pinned down at
    the tables
what sleight of hand we are forced to use
and
how heavily armed are the players
that play against us
according to rules which they change
from card to card

And on the wall is written:
'Only he who fights back is a man'
so that they can
lawfully shoot us down

The German phrase 'um die Ehre' (lit. 'for honour') is the equivalent
of the English 'for love' i.e. without stakes.

Transformation

My girl-friends turn slowly
over three or four weeks
or quickly over night
into my aunts and old cousins

I see them chew anxiously
at their dentures
and with gouty fingers dry
the spittle from their faces

With cases and bundles
they arrive in Theresienstadt
They fumble for their glasses
as they fall from the window

Curled up in bed
they try to come to attention
so as to be spared
when they weed out the sick

When I kiss them in the morning
I see their bluish tint
piled six high
washed clean with garden-hoses

of shit and vomited slime
ready for transport
from the gas-chamber
to the cremation oven

Theresienstadt or Teresin was a concentration and extermination
camp, mainly for old people.

Paradise Lost

When I had lost
my first country
and when in my second country
and in my place of refuge
and in my third country
and in my second place of refuge
I had lost everything
then I set out

to look for a land
that was not poisoned
by any memories
of irreplaceable losses

So I came to Paradise
there I found peace
Everything was whole and good
I lacked for nothing

Then a sentry
with a flaming sword
said: 'Get away
Here you have lost nothing'

The Brink

I have always believed
that fear has a brink
where one can stand and look down
see how it coils
or makes bubbles
or smiles or stinks
and rots before our eyes

A brink
of which one knows
that it is to be feared
that one must not take a step further
nor lean over
that it is best to take
a couple of steps back
for even if the brink
is a balustrade one can hold on to
it is not to be trusted
it could be delapidated
and crumble or collapse

I have never believed
that it is solid
but did think of it
as a kind of warning sign
'So far and no further'
or 'Not quite so far'
and even in my nightmares
which showed me
how treacherous it can be
I still believed
that fear has a brink

I don't know why I believed it
but it was a comfort

On Ice

I have striven to be understood
and tried to speak
so that what I talk about
and my reasons for speaking
and my purpose
should be clearly heard
by those to whom I spoke

But what did they make of it?

I remember a joke
in which a child
who came late to school
blamed the black ice on the roads
For each step forward
he said
he had slipped
two steps back

Not so unlike my own case

'Then how did you get here at all?'
asked the teacher
'That's easy—I gave up
and just tried
to go back home'

Not so unlike my own case now

I will try
not to strive any more
to be understood
only to get back to myself
to the place where I was at home
and which now
isn't there any more

The joke about the ice
made me laugh
as a schoolboy

That I still remember clearly

Conservation of Matter

Every morning
I am embalmed

the mouth is rinsed out
with bitter essences

the dreams are forgotten
the hair combed

the teeth cleaned
the eyes opened wider

In the mirror before shaving
a deep breath is taken

after shaving
the skin of the face is rejuvenated

with spirit
and the hair with an atomiser

courage is taken
something warm gets into the stomach

Then I disintegrate
towards the next morning

A Man without Matches

All the things
that pretend
I have lost them
secretly gather
and arrange themselves
all on their own
into a house
with rooms ready furnished

It smells of bread already
in the kitchen
In our warm bed
you
really you
throw back the clothes
and naked stretch out to me
so that I can move in
two living arms

The German title refers to the little matchgirl of Hans Christian
Andersen's fairy-tale.

A Collector

The things I found
But they'll scatter them again
to the four winds
as soon as I am dead

Old gadgets
fossilised plants and shells
books broken dolls
coloured postcards

And all the words
I have found
my incomplete
my unsatisfied words

What It Is Made Of

My death is made of coins
and of paper money

My death is made of ways
to school and to work

My death is made of a time-clock
and of duties

My death is made of newspapers
and of policemen

of cigarettes and spirits
of sugar and bread and butter

of happy and unhappy love
of anger and patience

My death is made of my parents
and of my children

of my failures
and of my successes

of my servitude
and of my freedom

of my company
and of my loneliness

of my disbelief
and of my belief

of my hope
and of my disappointment

of my thinking
and of my forgetting

My death is made of my sex
and of my heart

My death is made of my nights
and of my days

My death is made of my waking
and of my sleep

of my life
and of your lives and deaths

In Sore Straits

Full of objects the world
which is made of objects

On the cupboard the suitcase
and above the suitcase the wall
and above the wall the ceiling with its
damp patch
and with its cobwebs
and near the cupboard the books
and above the books the picture
and above the picture a second picture
and on the frame the dust
and above that the place
where at Christmas
the paper-chain still hung
on a drawing-pin

a round black drawing-pin hole in the wall
but too small to bury the dead

Objects
surround me and really
become objects
that object to me
on all sides and leave me
no space any more

The room has got smaller
since the objects
began to gang up
but the distance
between the mouth that says so
and the ears
that don't want to hear
has got bigger

Perhaps in this way a hole will appear
different from the one in the wall

**Navigare necesse est,
vivere non est necesse.**

(Hanseatic saying)

To drift
on this ship
into the tropic of rages

whose rages
and rages
against whom?

Of those made into non-persons
of those turned into ghosts
for whom I could never

set out
enough
bowls of milk

to appease them
because
there is not enough milk

In the tropic of rages
perhaps
of rages against myself

because I drift
on their tide
and hardly attempt

any more to steer
this ship
this jangling wreck

Kitchen-Table-Talk

Between cutlery and crockery
leftovers of conversation
paraphrases yawns squabbles
winged words

But they do not fly
Nothing soars up and away
The bird hops away from me
and cowers under the drain-pipe

If I were dead
I'd want to hammer
at your
barred and bolted world

if I were
born again
find you
and speak to you

But I am living
and my words
don't reach you
and fall under the table

A Love Poem for Freedom and a Freedom Poem for Love

With freedom
it's much the same as with love

Suppose after all these years what they call happiness
takes me out of the locked cupboard again

and says: 'Have another go!
Let's see how you manage'

Shall I then breathe in deeply and open my arms
and be young again and full of courage

or shall I smell of moth-balls and rattle my bones
to the rhythm of a stranger's heart-beat?

With freedom
it's much the same as with love

and with love
it's much the same as with freedom

Freedom of Thought

When I think of your mouth
as you tell me something
then I think
of your words
and your thoughts
and the expression
of your eyes
as you speak

But when I think of your mouth
as it rests on mine
then I think
of your mouth
and of your mouth
and of your mouth
and of the lips of your sex
and of your eyes

What is Life?

Life
that is the warmth
of the water in my bath

Life
that is my mouth
on the open lips of your sex

Life
that is anger
at the wrongs in our countries

The warmth of the water
is not enough
I must also splash in it

My mouth on your sex
is not enough
I must also kiss it

Anger at wrongs
is not enough
we must also probe them

and do
something about them
only that is life

WHO RULES HERE?

French Soldiers Mutiny—1917

For years the troops have gone
like lambs to the slaughter

but these are bleating
They are marching through the town

They are marching
and they are bleating like sheep

By bleating they cease to be
a herd of sheep

Mutinying French soldiers did actually bleat as a protest.

Death Certificate

'Because it's all no use
They do as they please anyhow

Because I don't want to get
my fingers burnt again

Because they'll just laugh:
it only needed you!

And why always me?
I'll get no thanks for it

Because no one can sort this out
One might only make things worse

Because even what's bad
may have some good in it

Because it depends how you look at it
and anyway whom can you trust?

Because the other side too
gets wet when it rains

Because I'd rather leave it
to those more qualified

Because you never know
what you let yourself in for

Because it's a waste of effort
They don't deserve it'

These are the causes of death
to write on our graves

which will not even be dug
if these are the causes

Toy on Target

1
Dropping
toys
instead of bombs
for the Festival of the Children

that
said the market researchers
will doubtlessly make
an impression

It has made
a great
impression
on the whole world

2
If the aeroplane
had dropped the toys
a fortnight ago
and only now the bombs

my two children
thanks to your kindness
would have had something to play with
for those two weeks

On the day of the Vietnamese 'Festival of the
Children' U.S. bombers dropped toys, even on villages where shortly
before children had been killed by their bombs.

Last Aid

In American gas-chambers
you can
read two admonitions
One for physical
and one for spiritual comfort

'If you want to shorten your agony
breathe in deeply'
and
'Turn to God
and He will turn to you'

The Reckoning

Five hundred and sixty-seven old men and children and
     women
shot in a village called My Lai or Song My

and in another village 'everything that ran
out of the burning huts brought down like clay-pigeons'

and girls first arrested and communally raped
by one man after another and then stabbed to death

and eleven hundred women and children from a village
     on the coast
loaded on junks and towed out to sea

until the junks foundered and then the tow-ropes cut
and those who still swam finished off with machine-pistols

and the calculation that a watch stolen
in a Saigon brothel was worth ten Vietnamese

for which reason ten Vietnamese civilians mending a hedge
were zapped off from a helicopter one two three . . .

and in the Mekong Delta 'since nothing had happened
     for ages'
the announcement that villagers could be used as moving
     targets

and a prisoner who would not talk
thrown from a helicopter to make two others speak

and when the My Lai incident was already common
     knowledge
another two hundred and forty women and children killed

on 12th December 69 in the village of
Bin-Du-Dong. These were all isolated cases.

Hear O Israel

When we were the persecuted
I was one of you
How can I remain one
when you become the persecutors?

Your longing was
to become like other nations
who murdered you
Now you have become like them

You have outlived
those who were cruel to you
Does their cruelty
live on in you now?

You ordered the defeated:
'Take off your boots'
Like the scapegoat
you drove them into the wilderness

into the great mosque of death
whose sandals are of sand
But they did not take upon them the sin
you wished to lay on them

The imprint of their naked feet
in the desert sand
outlasts the traces
of your bombs and your tanks

During the 1967 Six Days War Egyptian soldiers who surrendered
were instructed by the Israelis to take off their shoes and walk home
across the hot desert sand.

Chile Again

They talk about Chile
and they are silent about Chile

Those who talk about Chile
disapprove of those
who are silent about Chile

and those who are silent about Chile
disapprove of those
who talk about Chile

Talk about Chile
is lost
in the silence about Chile

And the silence about Chile
is lost
in talk about Chile

And time passes
in Chile
and does not pass

Aufforderung zum Vergessen

'Wenn sie doch ihre alten Ansprüche endlich vergessen wollten!'—
Zionistisches Argument

Sei nicht dumm
sagt der Wind
Die Welt dreht sich weiter
Alles ändert sich
Das Gewesene muß man vergessen

Wenn du dein Feld vergessen könntest
sagt die vergiftete Ernte
und wenn du dein weißes Haus vergessen könntest
sagt der Schutt
und wenn du den großen Krug vergessen könntest
sagen die Scherben
und wenn du den Ölbaum vergessen könntest
sagt der Baumstumpf
und die Orangenbäume
sagt der verbrannte Hain

und wenn du deine zwei Schwestern vergessen könntest
sagt der Weg zu den Gräbern
und wenn du die Schreie vergessen könntest
sagen die Ohren
dann könntest du aufhören dich in Gefahr zu begeben
dann könntest du weit wegfahren wie die Dattel im Bauch
     eines Schiffes
die gepflückt wurde und die frei ist von ihrem Baum
dann könntest du frei sein wie ein Sandkorn im Wind
endlich frei von der Heimat
die du verloren hast

Die Welt dreht sich weiter
Das Gewesene muß man vergessen
Sei nicht dumm
sagt der Wind
der herweht von deinen Vertreibern

Invitation to Forget

'If only they would finally forget their old demands!' —
Zionist argument

Don't be stupid
says the wind
The world goes on turning
Everything changes
One must forget what has been

If you could forget your field
says the poisoned crop
and if you could forget your white house
says the rubble
and if you could forget the brown pitcher
say the shards
and if you could forget the olive-tree
says the tree-stump
and the orange trees
says the burnt grove

and if you could forget your two sisters
says the path to the graves
and if you could forget the screams
say the ears
then you could stop courting danger
then you could sail for away like a fig in a ships' belly

that has been plucked and is free of its tree
then you could be free like a grain of sand in the wind
free at last
of the native land you have lost

The world goes on turning
One must forget what has been
Don't be stupid
says the wind
blowing across from those who drove you away

39

Vielleicht Allende

Ich bin der Niederlagen müde
und müder noch
der Freunde die kommen nach jeder Niederlage
und beweisen: 'Eigentlich war sie ein Sieg'

Dabei reden sie so
um nicht selber der Niederlagen
so müde zu werden daß sie ihnen erliegen
Doch solche Reden
führen zu solchen Siegen

Ich weiß: Noch immer hing der Sieg des Neuen
am Ende einer Kette von Niederlagen
(von denen dies eine ist) als letztes Glied
Das könnte ein Trost sein
aber die Glieder bluten

Wenn ich tot bin können sie sagen:
'Er hat sich selbst getötet'
fast wie man sagen könnte
wenn ich das wirklich täte:
'Die ihn getötet haben das waren sie'

Aber wenn ich auch müde bin des Erlebenmüssens
ihrer Verbrechen und des Zeitungsgeschwätzes
diese Niederlage beweise die Vergeblichkeit unserer Sache
und müde meines Zualtseins um selbst noch die Kräfte
zu sammeln zum neuen Kampf
ich bin nicht müde des Kampfes
gegen die die eines Tags sterben
an meinem Tod

Allende Perhaps

I am tired of defeats
but tireder still
of friends who come after each defeat
and prove: 'Actually it was a victory'

They talk like that
so as not to be so tired of defeats
that they succumb to them
But that kind of talk
leads to that kind of victory

I know: The victory of the new
has always come at the end
of a chain of defeats
(of which this is one) as the last link
That might be some comfort
but links bleed

When I am dead they can say:
'He killed himself'
just as you could say
if I really did so:
'They were the ones who killed him'

But even if I am tired of having to endure
their crimes and the newspaper gossip
that this defeat is proof
of the hopelessness of our cause
and tired of being too old
to summon up the strength myself
for new struggles
I am not tired of the fight
against those who one day will die
of my death

The Return

Attica State Prison New York USA

For nine months
before the state police came
and opened fire
in Attica penitentiary
prison doctors said

to sick
Puertoricans
who understood only Spanish
'First learn English
then you can come back'

It is difficult
to learn English
when you are dead
But they will come back
for sure

Stalin on the Journey to Prague 1977

For example this prison wall—
Look at it
from the inside
then you'll see at once whom it serves
socialism
or the old order

If you don't see that
then you haven't
piercing eyes
like those I once had
then you have no right to have eyes
except for the last right
to see your own errors

But whether or not the wall
is part of our achievement
or of our heritage
whether it was saved only
because earmarked
for our new ends
it is useful
but it is imperfect

It can crumble
through the work of wreckers within
or on account of amnesties
which though tactically necessary
nevertheless set enemies free
at least
until we rearrest them

More effective than this wall
was its expeditious brother
the bullet in the back of the neck
which came after the confession
that always remained true—
however obtained—

because like the final shot
it served the good cause
the strategy of the future
death for the sake of life

To call the bullet in the back of the neck
by its right name
many believe is a tactical error
But comrades what was it?
Our bullet in the back of the neck
was a form of struggle
in fact a conclusive one
against internal enemies
and a weapon from our arsenal

But since the enemy has been speaking about it
trying to confuse us with phrases
more and more walls are needed
to protect the masses
at least
until we introduce the old method

Feeble time of transition
in which I lie buried
without mausoleum
but without a stake through my heart

Stalin on the Journey to Prague 1977: The title is a reference to Mörike's
novella *Mozart's Journey to Prague.* 1977 refers to the Charter
produced in that year in Czechoslovakia.

The Freedom to Open One's Mouth

The freedom to open one's mouth
exists even when
some people proclaim
'They are being made to shut up'

On the contrary
You need simply make a list of all
that comes out of mouths
that seem to be shut

Firstly screams
secondly right at the start
and perhaps at the very end
still some protests

thirdly teeth and fourthly blood
and fifthly vomit and sixthly
in many cases liquids
introduced through tubes or by immersing the head

You mustn't be narrow-minded
for the freedom to open one's mouth
means the same right for everyone
for example the warders

to force open the stubborn mouth
of a prisoner
What goes into it?
A lot of oil and a lot of water

Or the heel of a boot
or urine or bloody rags
or shit
or sawdust or earth

And what comes out
if all goes well
is the
voluntary confession

The mouth often suffers
but never the freedom to open one's mouth
that still obtains—one way or another—
in all our lands

In the Capital

'Who rules here?'
I asked.
They said:
'The people naturally'.

I said:
'Naturally the people
but who
really rules?'

On Inner Freedom

I bent down
to kiss
the gleaming black boots
of our master
then he said:
Lower

As I bent lower
I felt within me
magnificently
the resistance
of my spine
not wishing to bend

Gladly I crept away
thankful to our master
for this experience
of my inner
power
and dignity

First Aid

After the next war
the three guardians will come
and render help everywhere
as best they may

One of them
will bring food to the ruins
which stretch out to him
their hungry towers

The second will
plant the gathered bones
so that they grow
and put on flesh again

which the first can use
to feed the ruins
for without flesh
they cease to be romantic

but the third guardian
will build from bushes and grass and paper
nests
for the stones and for their children

Rückblick

Ich wollte
meiner Zeit
Flamme sein
oder
Teil ihrer Flamme

Ich war
ihr Schatten
oder
ein Teil
ihres Schattens

Meine Zeit
war die Zeit
der Wut:
Schatten der Wut.

Meine Zeit
war die Zeit
der Ohnmacht:
Schatten der Ohnmacht

die Zeit
der Tyrannei:
Schatten der Tyrannei

Ich wollte
meiner Zeit
Fahne sein
oder ein
Fetzen der Fahne

Fahne
der Flamme
der Wut
der Ohnmacht
der Tyrannei
oder ihr Fetzen
oder ein Teil
seines Schattens

Retrospect

I wanted
to be the flame
of my time
or
part of its flame

I was its shadow
or
part
of its shadow

My time
was the time
of fury—
shadow of fury

My time
was the time
of helplessness—
shadow of helplessness

the time
of tyranny—
shadow of tyranny

I wanted
to be the banner
of my time
or a shred of its banner

Banner
of flame
of fury
of helplesnesss
of tyranny
or its shred
or part
of its shadow

Revolution

She devours her children
she drinks the blood of her dead
she preaches to the deaf
she knows no higher laws

She forgets her way
she reels from betrayal to betrayal
from error to error
she sleeps in her defeats

That she is unnecessary
every child learns at school
that the people don't want her
the people have grasped at last

That she can't win
has been proved ten times over
Those who have furnished the proof
do not sleep well

Those who believe in her
are often weary with doubts
A few of those who hate her
know she is coming

Clean Sweep

The causes
now fight
their effects

so that one can no longer
hold them
responsible for the effects

for even
to make them responsible
is part of the effects

and effects are forbidden
and punished
by the causes themselves

They do not wish
any longer
to know about such effects

Anyone who sees
how diligently
they pursue the effects

and still says
that they are
closely connected with them

will now have to
blame
only himself

Because thou art lukewarm

Those who are
for wars
without horror
for executions
without cruelty
for sentences
without executions
for imprisonment
without beatings
for interrogations
without torture
for torture
without lasting damage
for exploitation
without unreasonable hardship
shall be blessed
without blessing
and shall be cursed
without curses

The Experts

There are times
when even opportunists
run down
opportunism

Believe them
because they know—
none better—
what they are talking about

Don't trust them
because they run down
opportunism
out of opportunism

What Happens

It has happened
and it goes on happening
and will happen again
if nothing happens to stop it

The innocent know nothing
because they are too innocent
and the guilty know nothing
because they are too guilty

The poor do not notice
because they are too poor
and the rich do not notice
because they are too rich

The stupid shrug their shoulders
because they are too stupid
and the clever shrug their shoulders
because they are too clever

The young do not care
because they are too young
and the old do not care
because they are too old

That is why nothing happens
to stop it
and that is why it has happened
and goes on happening and will happen again

Prayer at Night

Model within us
or of us
in which we still find some meaning
help us
so that we neither intone nor echo
the false doctrines
of the elctronic brains
and their masters and servants

Where injustice becomes greater than we are
where injustice becomes swifter than we are
where injustice becomes stronger than we are
help us not to tire

Where injustice excels us
in knowledge and resources
where injustice excels us
in endurance and success
where injustice becomes so great
that we shrink
at its glance
help us not to despair

When injustice invades us
in our days and nights
in our startled waking and in our dreams
in our hopes and in our curses
help us
not to forget ourselves

Where injustice speaks with the voices
of justice and of power
where injustice speaks with the voices
of benevolence and of reason
where injustice speaks with the voices
of moderation and of experience
help us not to become bitter

And if we do despair
help us to see that we are desperate
and if we do become bitter
help us to see that we are becoming bitter
and if we shrink with fear
help us to know that it is fear
despair and bitterness and fear

So that we do not fall
into the error
of thinking
we have had a new revelation
and found the great way out
or the way in
and that alone had changed us

P²: POETRY ABOUT POETRY

P²: In his notebooks the German poet, critic and scholar, Friedrich Schlegel wrote: p for poetry
                              p² for poetry about poetry
                              p³ for poetry about poetry about poetry

One Sings

One sings
out of fear
against fear

One sings
out of danger
against danger

One sings
out of his time
against his time

One sings
out of the dust
against the dust

One sings
of the names
that make names nameless

Those with the words

I envy those with the grand words
they talk about the people
as if there were people
they talk about the fatherland
as if there were a fatherland
and about love and courage and cowardice
as if there were such things
as courage cowardice love
and they talk about fate
as if there were such a thing as fate

And I admire those with the cutting words
they talk about the people
as if there were no people
and about the fatherland
as if there were no fatherland
and of love and courage and cowardice
as if it were obvious
that there are no such things
and they talk about fate
as if there were no such thing as fate

And at times I don't know
whom I envy and whom I admire
as if there were only envy and no admiration
or as if there were only admiration and no envy
as if there were only grandness and no sharpness
or as if there were only sharpness and no grandness
and then I do not know
whether there is such a thing as talking and knowing
or as being or such a thing as myself
All I know is this does not work

Poetical Allusion

Only the fragment
do you allow
a puzzle of splinters
you throw down to us
as a hint
that something
must have
been broken

Long
before we
guess
what
and
by whom
you are gone

The Prophet

(on Khalil Gibran's The Prophet)

The prophet said:
'Only when you drink of silence
will you truly sing
Only when you reach the mountain-top
will you begin to climb
Only when the earth embraces you
will you truly dance'

They made you drink
from the river of silence
but you did not sing
They drove you up
to the highest mountain-top
but you climbed no further
The earth has embraced
your limbs
but you do not dance

The prophet was a false prophet
he erred
or he lied

Those who drowned our dead
did not teach them
to sing
Those who cast down our dead
did not teach them
to climb
Those who bulldozed earth onto our dead
were not their dancing-masters
but their murderers

The murderers still sing
words that have barely changed
to the old tune
The murderers still climb

from peak
to higher peak
The murderers dance over graves
and dungeons

Smilingly the murderers
tolerate the saying of the prophet
that still
makes everything
beautiful

Fragen nach der Poesie seit Auschwitz

Ob sie aufstieg als braunes Vöglein
aus dem Rauch der Verbrennungsöfen
und dann Rast hielt auf einer der Birken
von Birkenau

Ob sie näherflog
angelockt von den Schreien der Mädchen
und bei der Vergewaltigung zusah
und dann

dem Staub der Ruinenstädte
ihr Lied sang von stiller Liebe
und den Verhungernden
die Ballade vom reifenden Korn

Ob sie aufwuchs im Schatten des Geldes
und ihm ihre Stimme lieh
weil es längst schon zu groß war
um noch klimpern zu können

Ob sie die Welt durchflog
und ihren Sinn für das Schöne
von den bunten Farben
der zerrissenen Körper lernte

vom hellen Brand der Dorfhütten
oder von Spiegelungen
des wechselnden Tageslichtes
in glasigen Augen

Ob sie in einem chemisch entlaubten Baum
zuletzt ihr Nest aus verschont gebliebenen Haaren
Papierfasern Kleiderresten
und blutigen Federn baute

Questions about Poetry since Auschwitz

Whether it rose up as a small brown bird
out of the smoke of cremation ovens
and then rested in one of the birchs
of Birkenau

whether it flew closer
drawn by the screams of the girls
and saw them raped
and then sang

to the dust of the ruined cities
its song of quiet love
and to the starving
the lay of the ripening corn

whether it grew up in the shadow of money
and lent it its voice
for money had grown too big
to be able to jingle

whether it flew through the world
and learned its sense of beauty
from the vivid colours
of bodies torn to pieces

from the bright flames of village huts
or from the glint
of the changing daylight
in glazed eyes

whether at last in a tree
stripped by defoliants
it built its nest of hair
of paper shreds of rags and bloody feathers

und nun auf Paarung wartet
auf das Sitzen auf ihren Eiern
und auf das Ausschlüpfen ihrer
immer wieder unschuldigen Jungen

das wissen nur lyrische Dichter
die unentwegten
Rufer zum Vogelschutz
in der bald wieder heilen Welt

and now waits for mating
for the time to sit on its eggs
and for the hatching of
its eternally innocent young

that only lyric poets know
who steadfastly call
for wild bird protection
in a world soon to be whole again

The title is a reference to the statement by Theodor
Adorno that no poetry is possible after Auschwitz.

Speechless

'Why do you
still
write poems
although
with this method
you still reach
only minorities?'

ask friends
impatiently
because with their methods
they too still reach
only minorities

and I don't know
how to answer
them

A Connoisseur of Women

There was a man once called the morning
'the yellow whore
small yet terrifyingly tough'

All right—
the man
is a poet
and perhaps thinks nothing of it
if he uses a woman
for that sort of metaphor

But I hope
that when a poet like that
some day happens to come
too near a whore again
she will wish him or give him
a very good morning
that will stay on in his system
small yet terrifyingly tough

Good Resolution

I've had enough
I have written too much
From now on I shall write only
what one isn't allowed to write

But it is not enough
if the rulers say to me
'That you must not write'
for they say too often one must not

No. I must also
ask my comrades
of this group and that
who no longer speak to each other

When they too say to me
'That you must not write'
I can begin to know
that I must write it

Engaged Poem

I remember
my anger
and my search
for the right words
for my anger
and the last revision
before the clean copy
and reading it aloud
and in the end
my satisfaction
which rid me of my anger

So I can afford to forget
how I fumbled in vain
for the white sheets of paper
and took fright
because my fingers
get clumsier
and because the carbon
for the clean copy
kept falling
and I felt giddy
when I picked it up

Questions from an Engaged Poet

How long will it take you
not to be indignant
at the things
I say?

And will I still be there
to say them?
And will it still help
if they are said?

Won't they be too obscure
or too self-evident
and won't I just croak:
'I said so all along'?

The Rebirth of Poetry

O splendour of Aesopean language
soon you will return to us.
Then we too shall be able once more with a good conscience
to mirror ourselves in all the ages about which we
have read enough to acquire the taste
and to melt them down on the slow fire
of our lives
to greasy references

Thanks be to the mighty who with their cunning statecraft
bar our way to the barrenness of simple expression
and enrich us
by leading us
to fraternise with other ages in which
almost as today caution gripped the hand of freedom

Now it is no longer necessary to think of anything new
or to describe anything more precisely than comes with
    ease
Now simply to hint with a touch of courage
at what all already know
earns warm applause
and the mighty permit the small fry their small comfort
and almost always tolerate
whatever gives breathing-space and does not endanger them

Our public
which could no longer be satisfied
they make sharp of hearing and grateful again
for the longing for freedom
when she whom we greatly love
lures us on still lightly veiled
is more beautiful than naked
shameless freedom herself
from which they thoughtfully protect us

Aesopean language is the language of slaves forced to resort to
allegories to convey the truth.

75

By the Sea

(*On Arthur Rimbaud's 'Marine'*)

They whip it
they whip it fast and loud
they who whip men women and animals
whip the foam

the foam they hope
will drown the foam of the waves
the spray that flew up weightless
to the moon
long before the first dreams
of astronauts

The chariot of silver and copper
the prow of steel and silver
the suprasonic plane
of mathematical formulae
and gleaming polished profits
they all help to whip it

They all help to whip the foam
but the foam is bloody
poisonous soap bubbles
whipped into towering ringlets
out of the water dirty from all the efforts
to wash us clean

Cold blood
flakes of red snow
on the endless furrows of the ebb-tide
on the pillars of the forest
I too wounded myself once
on the blade of the vortex of light

Is there still hope then
that I too may not
begin to foam
but once more see
the foam of the surf?
the foam of the waterfall?
Is there really hope
that the world will last longer
than all these wounds from the whips of men?

Hölderlin an Sinclair

Was ist geblieben?
Nichts mehr und alles. Nämlich,
Was war, das ist und wird sein,
Auch gegen sich selbst.
Zuviel aber ist umsonst,
Und was mir schien,
Scheint nicht länger.

Aber des Todes ist wenig.
Denn sind auch verheert
Die Brunnen im Land
Und abgeholzt an den Straßen
Die heiligen Bäume des Seins,
Es kann doch keinem
Auferlegt werden, alles
Mitanzusehen, daß er es ewig ertrage
Ohne Empörung, selbst um der Liebe willen.
Und ist erst entzündet
Der Mut, so wächst ihm auch Mitleid
Mit denen, die,
Gescheucht in den Schutz der Schatten,
Versäumen den eigenen Zorn.

Viel kann verstört sein,
Daß der suchende Blick es
Kaum noch erkennt.
Nicht alle Vögel, die singen,
Helfen dem Himmel. Doch wo
Gesang fehlt, dort erblindet
Der arme Gefangene.
Das letzte aber ist Leben.

Hölderlin to Sinclair

What remains?
Nothing more and everything. Namely
What was, is and will be
Even in spite of itself.
But too much is in vain
And what once seemed to me
Seems so no longer.

But death shall have little.
For though the wells of the land
Are laid waste
And hewn at the roadside
The sacred trees of being,
This can be laid on no man
That he watch and bear things for ever
Without revolt, even for love's sake.
But once courage is kindled
Then compassion too grows in him
For those who
Herded into the shelter of the shadows
Miss their moment for anger.

Many things may be confused
So that the questing glance
Barely knows them again.
Not all birds that sing
Give help to heaven. But where
Song fails there blindness comes
To the poor prisoner.
Yet the last of all is life.

Sinclair was Hölderlin's friend and benefactor. They were both
involved in 'Jacobin conspiracies'.

Adaptation

Yesterday I began
to learn to speak
Today I am learning silence
Tomorrow
I shall stop learning

GERMANY—POLITICAL

Thousand-Year-long Empire

The guardians of the constitution
eat
of the tree
of their knowledge

and rooted in blood
and soil
richly dunged
with taxpayers' money
and servility

the tree flourishes.
The more they pluck
the more knowledge
it bears

Thus they are
as God
knowing
good and evil

At least like his angels
destroying angels
angels of silence
angels with swords
sentinel angels
guardian angels
(angels to guard
state and constitution)

Everywhere angels
with swords
that spurt rapid fire
and stop
all mortals
from storming their paradise
They themselves ensure
heavenly peace and order

so that lion and lamb
lie down together
tamed
by the same
accidental shot
aimed to kill
in self-defence
especially against the lamb

1) 'guardians of the constitution' is a translation of *Verfassungsschützer*,
the West German secret police, who refer to the results of their
investigations as *Erkentniss*, i.e. knowledge (cf. *Baum der Erkentniss* —
the tree of the knowledge of good and evil).
2) 'angels of silence' — the angels depicted on posters by Goebbels
during the 2nd World War as a warning against careless talk.

Thirty Years On

Incautiously
I begin
to remember

More cautiously
they begin
to forget me

Two are Shouting

The one is listened to
the other is not

The one they calm down
they engage him in debate
The other is still shouting
they walk over to him and smile

They ask through a megaphone:
'Why don't you shut your big mouth?'
'Listen!' he shouts 'Then you'll hear!'
They reply: 'We can't hear a word'

He is still shouting
They bring him the one
who no longer shouts
only opens and shuts his mouth

They call out to the other:
'*This* is the way to shout!
This we can all hear!
This is what we find stirring!'

They lead away the one
The other one is still shouting
They close the road
so that no one hears him

They bring him a newspaper
with his picture
Underneath the caption:
'Our soundless bigmouth'

He tries to shout still louder
he drops down and is dead
The other one is instructed
to whisper the last oration

Questions and Answers

Where has freedom gone?
To the four winds
And democracy?
To the dogs and to jail

Where has hope gone?
Into the constitution
And disenchantment?
Into its interpetation

Who listens to justice?
Where may it live?
When will freedom return?
To whom is it sacrificed?

Where have the questions gone?
To the scissors
What did they give us?
Nothing but paper

Where have the answers gone?
To the machine-pistols
What did they give us?
Dead and dead and more dead

The Basic Law of the Federal Republic guarantees freedom
from discrimination on the grounds of a person's views; in 1975,
however, the Constitutional Court ruled that this freedom referred
only to *having* particular views not to uttering or spreading
them.

A Question of Definition

Is a democracy
in which one may not say
that it is not
a real democracy
really
a real democracy?

Weaker

They are getting stronger again
Who is?
They are

Who should they be?
They should not be
they just are

Stronger than who?
Than you
soon perhaps than many

What do they want?
First of all
to get stronger again

Why do you say all this?
Because I can still
say it

Can't this get you into trouble?
Yes
for they are getting stronger

What makes you so sure?
Your own words
that I can get into trouble

Tiermarkt—Ankauf

Der Polizeipräsident
in Berlin sucht:
Schäferhundrüden.

Alter ein bis vier Jahre,
mit und ohne
Ahnentafel.

Voraussetzungen: einwandfreies Wesen
rücksichtslose Schärfe
ausgeprägter Verfolgungstrieb

Schußgleichgültig
und
gesund

Überprüfung
am ungeschützten Scheintäter
Hund mit Beißkorb

Gezahlt werden
bis zu
750,-- DM

Angebote an:
Der Polizeipräsident
in Berlin W-F 1

1 Berlin 42
Tempelhofer Damm 1-7
Tel. 69 10 91

Apparat
27 61
Strich 64

Wanted—Animals

The Berlin
Chief of Police
wants:
Alsatian dogs

Age one to four years
with or without
pedigree

Must have impeccable character
strong hunting instinct
and be ruthlessly fierce

Not gun-shy
and
healthy

Tests carried out
on unprotected mock criminal
dogs muzzled

Will pay
up to
750 Deutschmarks

Offers to:
The Chief of Police
Berlin W-F 1

1 Berlin 42
Tempelhofer Damm 1–7
Telephone 89 10 91

Extension 2761
Stroke 64

The poem reproduces the text of an advertisement by the Berlin
Chief of Police.

Regulations for Mourning

It is forbidden
to mourn for persons
who had different views
from the mourner himself

firstly because
our human compassion
is far too precious a gift
to be squandered like that

secondly because mourning
for those who think differently
has hampered surveillance
of our society

so that even criminal mourning
has gone scot-free with the excuse
that the mourner did not
think like the deceased

But since no one really
thinks exactly like anyone else
it is best
to mourn only oneself

That kind of mourning
can be all the more genuine and deep
and given the help of the state
all the more inconsolable

No one must fear
that there will be a lack of occasions
if mourning is confined
to an ever smaller circle

On the contrary—
only where no one mourns others
will everyone have
sufficient reason to mourn himself

Soap Bubbles

I clutched
at a straw
and blew
politicians
generals
and policemen

Once blown up
they shimmered
in every colour
but burst
as soon as you
touched them

A policeman
whom I told about it
without touching him
touched me
with his truncheon
so that I burst

The Innocent

I have laughed
the way one laughs
and shrugged my shoulders
the way one shrugs one's shoulders
and talked and been silent
the way one talks and is silent
and have not wept
the way one doesn't weep

So why shouldn't I live
the way one lives?

The Cunning of Reason

We know
that it
is the cunning
of reason
but does it know it?

Does this knowledge
make us more cunning
or more reasonable
than it is?

Do we outdo it
in reason
or has it
more cunning
than we?

The Cunning of Reason refers to Hegel's concept: Die list der Vernunft

Verdammungsurteil

für Ulrike Meinhof

1
Sie wurde zum
politischen Wahnsinn
getrieben
von den politisch
Normalen
und deren Normen

2
Wenn sie noch schreiben könnte
sie selbst müßte ihn schreiben
den endgültigen Bericht
über ihren Tod

und die Selbstmordbeweise
sichten
und einzeln
erwägen

und sagen
wer
diesen Selbstmord
begangen hat

Condemnation

Ulrike Meinhof

1
She was driven to
political madness
by the
politically normal
and their norms

2
If she could still write
she herself would have to write
the definitive report
on her death

and review
the evidence for suicide
and weigh it
bit by bit

and say
who it was
that committed
this suicide

The Man of Inaction

I do nothing

I know nothing

I do not know
that I do nothing

I do not want to know
that I know nothing and do nothing

I do not want to know
that I do not want to know
that I want to do nothing

I do not want to know
that I do not want to do
what I am not doing

I do not want to know
that I do not want to know
that I do not want to do
what I am not doing

I want to do everything
not to have to know
that I do not want to do
what I am not doing

I want to know everything
that I have to know
and have to do
to that end
So how can anyone say
that I do not want to know or do anything?

COMRADES?

Winter Bivouac

And the cheerful fires
what has become of them all?
Those who question sit shivering
in twos and threes and
the cold shines bright

I clasp my arms over my breast
I clasp my breast over my heart
I clasp my heart over my fear
layer upon layer upon layer
and inside
who knows?

An onion that barely survives the winter
and the cold cuts it up and must weep
The clever ones chew grimly over the pungent fare
And the cheerful fires
what has become of them all?

Learning Process

I am nothing
I am the lowest of the low
in our revolution
cried the engaged artist

They repeated after him:
You are nothing
you are the lowest of the low
in our revolution.
Then he was disenchanted

Needs Must

Today alas
we have not time
for the finer things of life

said someone
whom years ago
I knew as a boor

In Hiding

I must learn to hide
from my persecutors
and am thereby
in double danger

Perhaps still not well enough
hidden from them
and perhaps by now
hidden too well from myself

Instructions on the Maintenance of Striking-Power

The more enemies the more honour

Enemies
are too distant
and mostly
too well protected

So call your friends
enemies
and bash in
their teeth

If in this way
you manage
to make them into enemies
then you can boast:

'I was the first
to stand up
and strike a blow
in the struggle against them'

Conflict between Sole Beneficiaries

My Marx will pull out
your Marx's beard

My Engels will knock out
your Engel's teeth

My Lenin will break every bone
in your Lenin's body

Our Stalin will shoot
your Stalin in the back of the neck

Our Trotsky will split open
your Trotsky's skull

Our Mao will drown
your Mao in the Yang-tse

so that he can no longer stand
in the way of victory

Fears and Doubts

Have no doubts
about the one
who tells you
he is afraid

but be afraid
of the one
who tells you
he has no doubts

Petty-bourgeois Weakness

Painful for me
sometimes
to feel myself alone
among comrades
but that is
naturally
not forbidden

though I
also know
some comrades
who would like
to forbid it
Among them
I feel alone

Revised Version

for Ernst Fischer

Imagine socialism
freed of everything
that upsets you

Ask yourself
who then would be
really upset

He and no other is
and remains
your real enemy

A Work of Enlightenment

He wanted
to show
that he had a right to do
what he had to do

he managed
But now
it is too late
to do it

Return on Investment

Gathering hope
from soluble problems
from anything
that has some promise

Saving up
energies
for
the job in hand

That is how
to accumulate quietly
a reserve
of unexpended despair

Nebensache

Beschäftigt mit meinem Kampf
gegen den Hauptfeind
wurde ich von meinem Nebenfeind
erschossen

nicht von hinten und heimtückisch
wie seine Hauptfeinde sagen
sondern nur von der Seite
auf der er schon lange stand

und entsprechend
seiner erklärten Absicht
die ich nicht bekämpft hatte
weil er zu unwichtig war

Darum brachte mich auch mein Tod
nicht in Verwirrung
Ich widme mich weiterhin einzig
dem Kampf gegen den Hauptfeind

A Side Issue

Busy with my fight
against the main enemy
I was shot
by the secondary one

not from behind nor treacherously
as his main enemies say
but only from the side
where he had long been standing

and in line
with his declared intention
which I did not counter
since he was too unimportant

That is why even my death
did not confuse me
I am still entirely dedicated to the fight
against the main enemy

Practical Work

To teach
the stammerers
to speak

I learned to stammer
as fluently
as one of themselves

Why
do they
beat me up now?

Washed Clean

I knew a man
whom I would have liked to forgive
that his hands
were not clean
but he insisted
on washing himself publicly
from head to foot
and then
with finger scrubbed carefully pink
pointing
at others

Then all
I could see on him
were those places
that had grown chapped and rough
from so much scrubbing

The Unapproachable

for Herbert Marcuse

He approaches freedom
from a direction
we are not used to

he approaches freedom
in a way
we don't like

He makes up
to freedom
what does he want of her?

Not another step
Get back
or we shoot

We protect freedom
from anyone
who comes too close to her

Two Statements

1 *The Officials of the Revolution*

The officials
of the
revolution
have as much feeling
for it
as officials have
in the way of duty

and they have
the proper
official attitude
whereby
they decide
who may
take part in the revolution

2 *Grounds for Loving One's Enemy*

When the obtuseness
of my friends
has worn me out
the nastiness
of my enemies
can sometimes still
give me
new strength

ALMOST FUNNY

Constructive Self-Criticism

My weakness was
my sense
of superiority

Now I have
overcome it
I am perfect

Liberation from Great Models

No less a person
than Leonardo da Vinci
teaches us:
'Whoever always quotes authorities
certainly uses his memory
but not
his reason'

Get that into your heads:
Up with Leonardo!
Down with authorities!

A Human View of History

Franco was a great man with many failings
but at bottom just a human being like any other.
Hitler was a great man with many failings
but at bottom just a human being like any other.
Stalin was a great man with many failings
but at bottom just a human being like any other.
Churchill was a great man with many failings
but at bottom just a human being like any other.
Napoleon was a great man with many failings
but at bottom just a human being like any other.
Torquemada was a great man with many failings
but at bottom just a human being like any other.
Luther was a great man with many failings
but at bottom just a human being like any other.
Genghis Khan was a great man with many failings
but at bottom just a human being like any other.
Mohammed was a great man with many failings
but at bottom just a human being like any other.
Nero was a great man with many failings
but at bottom just a human being like any other.
Caesar was a great man with many failings
but at bottom just a human being like any other.
Alexander was a great man with many failings
but at bottom just a human being like any other.
Moses was a great man with many failings
but at bottom just a human being like any other.

How coloured and varied they seem
the figures of world history
if we look at them accurately
with sympathy and without prejudice

Classical Freedom of Choice

In the Mediterranean
cradle of our culture
one was free to choose
between Scylla
and Charybdis

Though it was said that the two
were secretly allied
most people would settle
for one
or the other

Strangely enough
not one of them
survived
except Odysseus
He did not recognise the need to choose

Market Day on Crete

The slavedealer had
a weakness for freedom
within the limits of the financially possible
and was almost always

full of good will towards
the people he had bought
wholesale from his pirates
and to whom he said:

'You and I
are in it together
without each other
none of us could live

for the pirates would
simply have thrown you overboard
if there were not men
of my profession

But I too have reason
to thank you
for my lucrative
socially useful calling

So help me and help yourselves
and tell me of your own free will
what you can do
and to whom you would rather be sold

Each according to his abilities!
Thus you will get
the best masters and
I the best price for you.'

Diogenes
who had fallen into the pirates' hands
on a voyage to Aegina
gave this answer:

'My benefactor
I know no profession
other than that
of ruling other men

so sell me to a man
who needs a master
Have no fear
You'll easily find such a man.'

The slavedealer
encouraged by these words
thanked Diogenes
and sold him

to Xeniades the Corinthian
who really did need a master—
that is
for his two sons—

Diogenes taught them
how unimportant riches and rank are
and how well slavery goes with
inner freedom

Carla M. born 5th May 1818

Since it was discovered
that Karl Marx
was really a woman
who set the fashion
with what was for her
a completely liberated relationship
with Friederich Engels
the attitude of the women's movement
to Marxism
is once again full of understanding
and lively interest

This revelation
about the case of Carla Marx
came just in time
to save the women
from getting bogged down
in a narrow-minded attitude

'A good point'
said the old comrade
'But leave out "narrowminded
attitude"

or else more women
will come along
and call our party loyalty
narrow-minded too

And without party loyalty
no democratic centralism
But you have told the women
where they get off

Carefree Artistic Temperament

In his circles
they take a good view of it
when you do
what people don't take a good view of

So of these things
people don't take a good view of
he only does those
they take a good view of in his circles

Pederasty as a Weapon

To the boy he had picked up
in the cinema André Gide confessed
in bed or next morning
after a night of love:

You can tell your friends
that you slept with a famous man
with an author.
My name is François Mauriac.

This poem is directed not against André Gide but at the common
political catchwords which speak of 'culture as a weapon' or 'poetry
as a weapon' or 'art as a weapon'.

The Salvation of the World

One day
all the dogs will gather—
those with blunt and those with pointed snouts
those with smooth and those with shaggy coats
those that can't stand the smell of each other
and those that can

At first they will still growl
and lift their hind-legs
all the dogs in the world at the same lamp-post
then they will wait
and then one will begin to bark

And then all the dogs
of all countries
will bark together
and then there will be peace at last

Many of them will bring their humans with them
but only prizewinners and only on the lead
They too can lift their legs
just like the dogs
and perhaps even
at the same lamp-post

but if any of them
starts another war
they will bite him to death

After an Old Soldier's Story

'How did you
take sixty prisoners
all by yourself?'

He laughed:
'Quite simple—
I surrounded them'

That's how I mean
to surround
the sixty lies

and the six hundred and sixty-six
dirty tricks
that master us

How
I don't know yet
but in the end it will be

quite simple
for there's no other way
And then I will laugh

THROUGH THE NET

Comparisons

Up turns to down
come turns to go
yes turns to no
good turns to bad
the night is deeper
than the night
the light is weaker
than the light

The road is longer
than the road
courage is smaller
than courage
fear is greater
than fear
death is nearer
than death

Fragen

fur Ivan Diviš

Wie groß ist dein Leben?
Wie tief?
Was kostet es dich?
Bis wann zahlst du?
Wieviel Türen hat es?
Wie oft
hast du ein neues begonnen?

Warst du schon einmal
gezwungen um es zu laufen?
Wenn ja
bist du rundherum gelaufen
im Kreis oder hast du
Einbuchtungen mitgelaufen?
Was dachtest du dir dabei?

Woran erkanntest du
daß du ganz herum warst?
Bist du mehrmals gelaufen?
War das dritte Mal
wie das zweite?

Würdest du lieber
die Strecke im Wagen fahren?
oder gefahren werden?
in welcher Richtung?
von wem?

Questions

for Ivan Diviš

How big is your life?
How deep?
What does it cost you?
How long do you have to pay?
How many doors has it?
How often
have you begun a new one?

Were you once
made to run for it?
If so
did you run round
in a circle
or did you run to and fro?
and what did you think to yourself?

How did you know
that you had come full circle?
Did you run more than once?
Was the third time
like the second?

Would you rather
drive that distance by car?
or be driven?
in what direction?
by whom?

Premonition of Final Victory

Sisyphus
dusty
and full
of the fine flour
of his stone
is afraid
The stone is wearing away

The senselessness
the eternally accursed
sense of his labour
is itself
struck by the curse

Smaller
like the dwindling stone
the mercy of the shades
that give him
the strength to be helpless

Soon only a pebble
will roll
on the flayed slope
What remains?

Nothing but the torture
to have outlived
his torture

Remarkable Child

The child with curls said
her hair was snakes
though invisible to others
they could spit
visible fire
that would burn up everything

No one was petrified
Instead they gave her
a truth drug that almost always
ensures that the patient
tells no lies

The story goes she took back nothing
The hospital burnt down

Die Herumgekommenen

Die Laute der fernen Küsten in ihren Ohren
sind nur Hafengeschrei
und Rasseln von Ankerketten
Schüttern von Zügen
Anfahren schwerer Loren
das Kreischen geschlagener Weiber
und das Röhren
der Schiffssirenen
zur Brunstzeit der christlichen Seefahrt

Und der Geruch fremder Länder in ihren Nasen
ist Schweiß und Staub
und halbverrauchte Gewürze
und Kinderurin in feuchten Quartieren
und Fusel
und Stadtstaub nach Sommerregen
und heiße Mauern am Abend
und Lack und Schmieröl
und billiges Hurenparfum

Und was sie für die Farben der Städte halten
die ihnen Augen machten
ist nur die blinde Farbe
ihrer Armut in allen Städten
und ihr Prahlen
mit ihren weiten Reisen
heißt nur:
Wir sind weit herumgekommen
in unserem Unglück

Old Salts

In their ears the sounds of distant coasts
are only shouts in a harbour
the rattle of anchor-chains
rumbling of trains
revving of heavy lorries
the screams of beaten women
and the belling
of ships' sirens
at the rutting-time of the navies of Christendom

In their noses the smell of strange lands
is sweat and dust
and half-stale spices
and children's urine in dank quarters
and rot-gut
and city dust after summer rain
and hot walls in the evening
and paint and grease
and cheap whore's perfume

And what they think are the colours of cities
making eyes at them
is only the blind colour
of their poverty in every city
And their boasting
about their long journeys
only means:
We have got about a lot
in our misery

The Investment

The spider falls silent
the wind sings in its threads
which still catch flies and bees
for its skeleton

The lighter it gets
the heavier the food hangs
full of nourishment
in the web
where the spider starved

Fairly Easily Cured

Noises that even in the dark
cannot be ignored
of the empty void
which envies
the full void

for its wealth
of journeys to the south
and of naked women
consumed as last course
after scampi and cheese and ice

The noise of hatred
with which the empty void
gnaws at the
colour slides
of the full void

That is why less well-off artists
must be kept under observation
by the authorities
Their vulgar envy
is so unpleasant

Fortunately it can be cured
by honours and prizes
and bathing alternately
in yellow girls
and brown boys

The void can be stuffed full
The void can be filled out
It is only with the double chins
that the voices become
eternal and mild

The last lines are a parodistic reference to Rilke's *Sonnets to Orpheus*
IX: Erst in dem Doppelbereich/werden die Stimmen/ewig und mild.
Literally: 'It is only in the double zone that the voices grow eternal
and mild.

141

Changeable weather

When the wind is right
the scent of paradise
gallops
towards us
Then we can pause for breath
long before our goal

But when the wind
is in our backs
the stench of corpses pursues us
and tarnishes with dew or frost
the tinsel haloes
of our riders

Suffering

This one suffers from his riches
and the other from his might
I suffer from seeing it all
as the day does from the night

This one suffers from loving
and the other from his need
I suffer from thinking of it
as life does from the dead

This one suffers from greediness
and the other from his lust
I suffer from my helplessness
as the heart does from the breast

Oxford Philosophy

1 *Non-intervention*

'Philosophy
leaves everything
the way
it is'

Then upon
the way it is
depends
the gravity of

its crime
in leaving everything
the way
it is

2 *'Importance is not important, truth is'*

J .L. Austin

His unimportant way
of dealing with importance
in truth
makes his truth
untrue

For how can truth
be important to him unless
it has some importance
But importance is
not important to him

3 *On the statement about the broom in the corner*

'My broom stands in the corner'
And what becomes of me
and of the room
and where has the dust come from
and is it really only dust?

And could the broom
even if it didn't
just stand there in the corner
still make a clean sweep of things?
where to?

'My broom stands in the corner'
Certainly
But where does the broom stand
of the one
that wants to sweep the world clean of me?

Is it still standing there?
Isn't it coming nearer?
From which corner?
And is there only one of them?

And shall the broom
in the corner
remain his broom
if he does not use it
to sweep out rubbish?

The Oxford philosopher
speaks only of what he knows
He answers calmly:
'My broom stands in the corner'

The New Subjectivity

Narrowing
one's horizon
so as to see more clearly
what has fallen
between the essentials
and has been lying there
under flakes of dust

Focussing
more and more sharply
until even the edge of the word
is too long
for the field of vision
and a mere two or three
of its notches
form a mountain range
in the glare
of renunciation
of the last image
that still includes objects

In this way with time
recognising
in an ever smaller field
more and more
of less and less
and in the end
seeing all
of nothing

Shrugging one's shoulders
at those old-fashioned people
who still hope
to widen their horizon
and though things blur
still to recognise
more and more
in broad outline
until they see no more
of everything

On the Eve

Broken pebbles of the days
Under the trees of the night
But the beasts of the evening wander and cry
Poor beasts of my lengthening evening
I'd like to stroke them
But they are timid

Death and life sway on equal scales
Ageing is a wind on the balance
a lazy fly
that hums through the nets of the south:
'Cast your reckoning
Use the useless time

Moisten the tongue that cleaves to your mouth
Go three steps back and hear what the scales' tongue says'
Only the useless flies
hum and buzz

only the beasts of the evening call and wander
under the trees of the night
beside the pebbles of the days
on the balance
between life and death